MATH IN OUR WORLD

USING
DIVISION FACTS
IN THE GARDEN

By Linda Bussell

Reading consultant: Susan Nations, M.Ed.,
author/literacy coach/consultant in literacy development
Math consultant: Rhea Stewart, M.A., mathematics content specialist

WEEKLY READER®
PUBLISHING

Please visit our web site at www.garethstevens.com
For a free color catalog describing our list of high-quality books,
call 1-800-542-2595 (USA) or 1-800-387-3178 (Canada). Our fax: 1-877-542-2596

Library of Congress Cataloging-in-Publication Data
Bussell, Linda.
    Division facts in the garden / by Linda Bussell.
        p. cm. — (Math in our world level 3)
    Includes bibliographical references and index.
    ISBN-10: 0-8368-9286-0 — ISBN-13: 978-0-8368-9286-4 (lib.bdg.)
    ISBN-10: 0-8368-9385-9 — ISBN-13: 978-0-8368-9385-4 (softcover)
    1. Division—Juvenile literature. 2. Gardening—Juvenile literature. I. Title.
QA115.B97   2008
513.2'14—dc22   2008012109

This edition first published in 2009 by
Weekly Reader® Books
An Imprint of Gareth Stevens Publishing
1 Reader's Digest Road
Pleasantville, NY 10570-7000 USA

Copyright © 2009 by Gareth Stevens, Inc.

Creative Director: Lisa Donovan
Designer: Amelia Favazza, Studio Montage
Copy Editor: Susan Labella
Photo Researcher: Kim Babbitt

Photo Credits: cover, title page: Ariel Skelley/Jupiter Images; pp. 4, 5, 7, 13, 19, 20: Hemera
Technologies; pp. 9, 11, 17: Photodisc, all other photographs by Gregg Andersen

Printed in the United States

1 2 3 4 5 6 7 8 9 10 09 08

Table of Contents

Words that appear in the glossary are printed in **boldface** type the first time they occur in the text.

Chapter 1

Fences First!

The Lewis School garden club plans a garden. They will grow vegetables. There are 27 students in the club. They **divide** into three groups. Each group has a job to do.

The first group plans the garden. The second group starts seedlings to plant later. The third group plans and builds a fence around the garden. The fence will keep animals from eating the plants. The fence must be built first. Then the students will plant the garden.

The group that will plan the fence meets. They meet with Miss Roberts. She is a teacher. She works with the garden club. The students discuss what they need to do.

"We must plan the fence," says Hannah. "First, we need to measure the outside of the garden. This will tell us how many feet the fence needs to be."

Danny says, "Yes. Then we can figure out how much **lumber** we need."

"That's right," says Miss Roberts.

To Do

- Measure the distance around the garden.
- Calculate how much lumber is needed.
- Buy lumber and supplies.
- Build fence.

After school, Danny's dad takes him to the home supply store. Hannah goes with them. They want to find the lumber they need.

Wood fences are made of **posts**, **rails**, and **slats**. Posts are thick pieces of wood. They go into the ground. They support the fence. Rails are attached to posts. Rails support the slats, or pickets. Slats are attached to the rails.

Hannah finds a catalog. It has pictures in it. She finds posts, rails, and slats. They can show this to the other students.

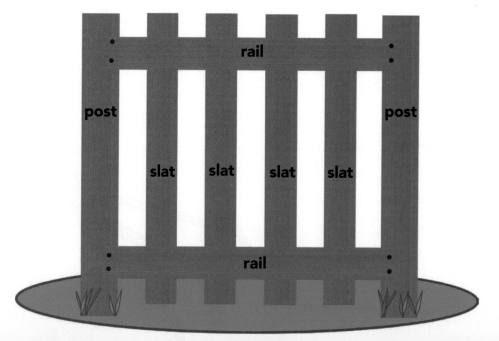

Chapter 2

Garden Division

The next day the club meets outside. They measure the distance around the edge of the garden. It is shaped like a rectangle.

The students use a tape measure. They work carefully. They want an accurate measurement.

Miss Roberts reminds them to check their work. They measure the distance around the garden again. It measures 88 feet both times.

"Good work," Miss Roberts says.

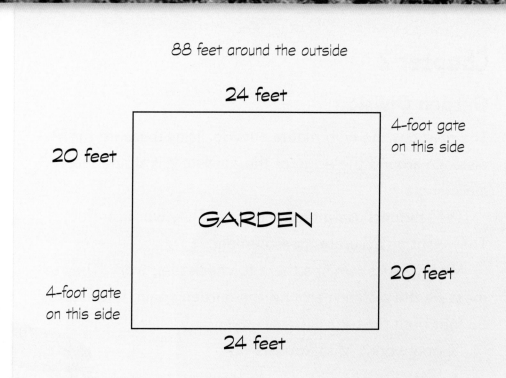

88 feet around the outside

24 feet

20 feet

4-foot gate
on this side

GARDEN

20 feet

4-foot gate
on this side

24 feet

The long sides of the garden are each 24 feet. The short sides are each 20 feet. There will be a gate along each short side. Each gate will be 4 feet wide. The students make a drawing of the garden.

Danny writes:

20 − 4 = 16

16 feet of fence for each short side

16 + 16 = 32

32 feet of fence for both short sides

24 + 24 = 48

48 feet of fence for both long sides

2 × 4 = 8

8 feet of gates

Danny shares his notes.

32 + 48 = 80
80 feet of fence

80 + 8 = 88
88 feet around the outside
of the garden

**Miss Roberts checks the
drawing of the garden
the students have made.**

"Good work," says Miss Roberts. "The distance around the garden is 88 feet. Your notes are correct. They are complete. We have the information we need now. We can plan the fence."

"We need to buy enough lumber to make a fence that is 80 feet long," says Hannah. "That does not include the gates."

The students will find the wood they need at a home supply store.

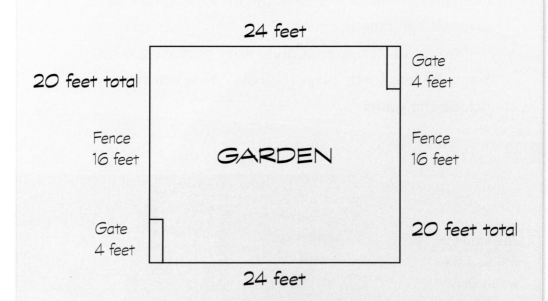

88 feet around the outside

24 feet

20 feet total

Gate
4 feet

Fence
16 feet

GARDEN

Fence
16 feet

Gate
4 feet

20 feet total

24 feet

"Each long side is 24 feet long," says Ms. Roberts. "How many 8-foot **sections** do we need for each long side?"

Hannah writes:

24 ÷ 8 = 3

3 rails on one long side

"We will not need to cut the rails," she answers. "We need 3 rails for each long side."

"The fence sections on the short sides are each 16 feet long," says Steve. "16 divided by 8 equals 2. We need 2 rails for each short side. We will not need to cut them either."

Chapter 3

Post It!

Hong looks at the catalog pictures again. "We forgot something!" she says. "We need rails on the top of the fence! We need rails on the bottom, too."

Miss Roberts smiles. "You are right. We need twice as many rails."

"We know how many rails we need. What about posts?" she says.

"We need a post every 4 feet," Miss Roberts says. "How many posts do we need for a 24-foot side?"

Hannah starts a list.

10 × 2 = 20
20 rails in all

The students figure out how many rails and posts they need for the garden fence.

Danny writes in his notebook.

24 ÷ 4 = 6

"We need 6 posts for each of the long sides," he says.
Hannah writes in her notebook, too.

20 ÷ 4 = 5

"We need 5 posts for each of the short sides," she says.
Then Hannah writes a number sentence.

6 + 6 + 5 + 5 = 22
22 posts in all

"We need 22 posts altogether."

	24 ÷ 4 = 6
	20 ÷ 4 = 5
	6 + 6 + 5 + 5 = 22

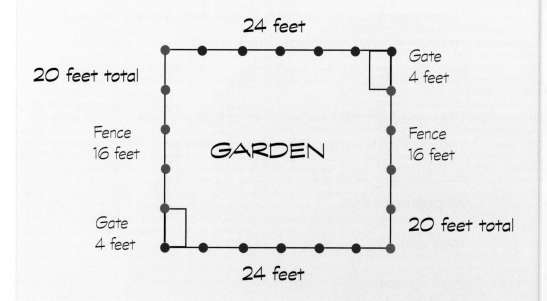

88 feet around the outside

24 feet

20 feet total

Gate
4 feet

Fence
16 feet

GARDEN

Fence
16 feet

Gate
4 feet

20 feet total

24 feet

"Let's color the posts in our drawing," says Danny. "The posts on the short sides can be red. The posts on the long sides can be blue."

"I count 6 posts on the long sides!" says Hong.

"I count 5 posts on the short sides," Steven says.

Hannah says, "Let's count the total number of posts."

There are 22 posts. That number is correct. Each of the sides shares a corner post with its neighbor.

The students figure out the number of slats they need. Miss Roberts says, "We need 16 slats to cover an 8-foot section."

Danny writes:

16 ÷ 8 = 2

Danny sums up all the information for the class.

- 20 rails
- 22 posts
- 160 slats
- 2 gates (4 feet each)

He says, "That means 2 slats cover 1 foot."

"Now we can calculate the number of slats we need," says Hannah. She writes:

80 feet of fence

2 slats per foot

80 + 80 = 160

"We need 160 slats," she says.

Now they are ready to buy the lumber. They already have nails, screws, and hardware.

Chapter 4

Harvest Time

A few months pass. The garden fence is done. It turned out well. The students planned. They measured. They bought the lumber. They built the fence. They are proud of their hard work.

The garden club plants its vegetable garden. They weed the garden. They water the plants. They build a scarecrow, too. The scarecrow keeps away birds. The fence keeps animals out of the garden. The plants grow well.

It is **harvest** time at last. It is time to pick the crops. There is an extra large crop this year! Everyone is pleased.

Each year the school has a festival. The students celebrate the harvest. They have food and games. The students serve the vegetables they grew in the garden.

Principal Stevens says, "This is the best harvest I can remember."

Miss Roberts is proud of the garden club!

The garden club shows the vegetables from their garden.

21

What Did You Learn?

(1) Twenty-seven students are cleaning up the park. There are 9 students in each group. How many groups of students are cleaning?

(2) Six girls bought 18 pieces of candy. If each girl bought the same number of pieces, how many pieces did each girl have?

(3) Mrs. Clark's math class has 33 students. Mrs. Clark must divide the class into 4 sections. Can each section have the same number of students?

Glossary

divide: to separate items into equal groups

harvest: the gathering of ripened crops

lumber: timber sawed or split into planks or boards

post: a piece of wood set upright into the ground for support

rail: a piece of wood, attached parallel to the ground between posts, that supports the slats

section: one of several parts of a whole

slat: a thin piece of wood used for fences

Index

About the Author

Linda Bussell has written and designed books, supplemental learning materials, educational games, and software programs for children and young adults. She lives with her family in San Diego, California.